P9-BYH-150

Word County Public Library

SAYINGS *and* PHRASES

Go Fly a Kite!

(And Other Sayings We Don't Really Mean)

written by Cynthia Klingel ★ illustrated by Mernie Gallagher-Cole

DISCARDED

ABOUT THE AUTHOR

As a high school English teacher and as an elementary teacher, Cynthia Klingel has shared her love of language with students. She has always been fascinated with idioms and figures of speech. Today Cynthia is a school district administrator in Minnesota. She has two daughters who also share her love of language through reading, writing, and talking!

ABOUT THE ILLUSTRATOR

Mernie Gallagher-Cole lives in Pennsylvania with her husband and two children. She uses sayings and phrases like the ones in this book every day. She has illustrated many children's books, including *Messy Molly* and *Día De Los Muertos* for The Child's World®.

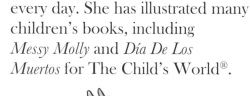

The Child's World®

Published in the United States of America by The Child's World®
1980 Lookout Drive • Mankato, MN 56003-1705
800-599-READ • www.childsworld.com

ACKNOWLEDGMENTS
The Child's World®: Mary Berendes, Publishing Director

The Creative Spark: Editing

The Design Lab: Kathleen Petelinsek, Design and Page Production

Copyright © 2008 by The Child's World®
All rights reserved. No part of this book may be reproduced or utilized in any form or by any means without written permission from the publisher.

LIBRARY OF CONGRESS CATALOGING-IN-PUBLICATION DATA
Klingel, Cynthia Fitterer.
Go fly a kite! (and other sayings we don't really mean) / by Cynthia Klingel.
  p. cm.—(Sayings and phrases)
  ISBN-13: 978-1-59296-904-3 (lib. bdg.: alk. paper)
  ISBN-10: 1-59296-904-6 (lib. bdg: alk. paper)
1. English language—Idioms—Juvenile literature.
2. Figures of speech—Juvenile literature. I. Title.
II. Series.
PE1460.K684 2007
428—dc22   2007004214

People use idioms *(ID-ee-umz) every day. These are sayings and phrases with meanings that are different from the actual words. Some idioms seem silly. Many of them don't make much sense . . . at first.*

This book will help you understand some of the most common idioms. It will tell you how you might hear a saying or phrase. It will tell you what the saying really means. All of these sayings and short phrases—even the silly ones—are an important part of our language!

TABLE *of* CONTENTS

An apple a day keeps the doctor away	4
An ax to grind	4
Back to square one	5
Beat around the bush	6
Beggars can't be choosers	6
Behind the scenes	7
Below the belt	7
Bite the bullet	8
Bolt from the blue	8
Burning the midnight oil	9
Bury the hatchet	9
Catch-22	10
Caught red-handed	11
A chip on your shoulder	11
Dead as a doornail	12
Down the hatch	12
Easy as falling off a log	13
Face the music	14
A flash in the pan	14
Full of beans	15
Go fly a kite	15
Have your cake and eat it too	16
Ignorance is bliss	17
Keep a stiff upper lip	17
Make ends meet	18
Miss the boat	18
On cloud nine	19
Out of the blue	19
Pit stop	20
Pull your hair out	20
Read the riot act	21
A shot in the dark	21
Spill the beans	22
Through the grapevine	22
Turn the tables	23
A wet blanket	24
X marks the spot	24

An apple a day keeps the doctor away

"Mom, I'm hungry!" yelled Hannah as she ran into the house. Her mother put a bowl on the table.

"Not apples again," groaned Hannah. "I had one for snack yesterday."

"Have another," answered her mother. "An apple a day keeps the doctor away!"

MEANING: Eating apples will help us stay healthy

An ax to grind

Joe wouldn't let Tom ride his new skateboard. Tom was always breaking things. One day Joe had soccer practice after school. Tom called Joe's brother, Ben. Tom asked Ben if he could come over. When Tom got there, he told Ben he had an idea.

"Hey, Ben! Let's skateboard," suggested Tom.

"But you didn't bring your skateboard," replied Ben.

"That's right," agreed Tom. "How about if I ride your brother's new one?"

Now Ben knew why Tom had come over. Tom had just wanted to ride Joe's new skateboard the whole time. Ben realized that Tom had an ax to grind.

MEANING: You pretend you want to do something, but you are doing it for a selfish reason

4

Back to square one

Holly baked cookies for the bake sale at school. Then she went to dance practice. When she came home, her little brother met her in the kitchen.

"Your cookies are really good, Holly!" he said. He'd eaten ten of them! Now there weren't enough cookies for the bake sale. Holly would have to make more. It was back to square one.

MEANING: To start something over again

Beat around the bush

Lucy had forgotten to do her homework. She was scared to tell her teacher the truth. She began thinking of excuses to tell Mrs. Lopez.

"Lucy, quit beating around the bush," said Mrs. Lopez. "Please just tell me the truth."

MEANING: To try not to answer a question or give a clear answer

Beggars can't be choosers

Rita didn't like the soup her dad had put in her lunchbox. Instead, she wanted the sandwich that Andy had.

"Hey, Andy. Want to trade me for your sandwich?" asked Rita.

"Sure. I'll trade. But you can only have half," said Andy.

"Half? Just half? But I want the whole thing!" complained Rita.

"Then forget it," replied Andy. "Beggars can't be choosers."

MEANING: When you can't have exactly what you ask for, you must accept whatever you can get and not complain.

Behind the scenes

Mike and Nicole were having a magic show for their friends. They did many different tricks. Doves appeared. Milk disappeared. Sparks flew into the air. The audience loved the show. They were surprised by all the magic things that happened. They clapped and clapped. What they didn't see was Mom and Dad behind the curtain. They had been busy doing things to make the magic tricks work.

"Thank you, everyone, for coming to our show," announced Mike.

"A special thank you to Mom and Dad," added Nicole. "We couldn't have done it without their work behind the scenes!"

MEANING: Something done out of sight of other people

Below the belt

During a game of tag, Abby tripped Tara. Then Tara got tagged. Abby started saying mean things about Tara not being a good runner. Bree heard Abby bragging.

"That's not fair, Abby," said Bree. "I saw you trip Tara. Saying those things is hitting below the belt. We don't want people playing who act like that."

"I'm sorry, Tara," said Abby. "I know you are a good runner. I won't do it again."

MEANING: To do something unfair or against the rules; to do something mean or unkind

Bite the bullet

Dad did not like cleaning the garage. It was always a mess. All morning he kept busy with other things to do. Finally, Jesse found Dad in the garden.

"Dad," said Jesse. "We're going skateboarding this afternoon. I thought you were going to clean the garage and help me find my skateboard."

"All right," replied Dad. "I guess I just need to bite the bullet and get started."

MEANING: To do something you don't want to do; to do something that is painful or hard

Bolt from the blue

George couldn't believe it. He had worked hard to be a good leader on his baseball team. He hoped to be voted captain this year. He was sure he would get it. The team voted. When the votes were counted, Jimmy had won. George was stunned. He told his uncle as soon as he got home.

"George, I'm sorry about what happened," his uncle said. "I know how much you wanted to be captain. You worked really hard for it. The vote for Jimmy must have been a bolt from the blue."

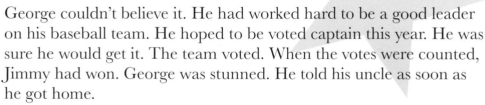

MEANING: When something completely unexpected happens. Often the unexpected thing is not good.

8

Burning the midnight oil

Dan was excited for the science fair. He had entered every year, but had never won. He wanted to win this year! This would be his best project ever. He worked on it every night. It was getting harder and harder to get up each morning when his alarm went off.

"Dan," called his mom one night. "Aren't you about finished with that project yet?"

"Almost," answered Dan. "A few more hours and I think I'll be done!"

"I'm glad!" exclaimed his mom. "You've been burning the midnight oil for the past two weeks."

MEANING: To stay up late

Bury the hatchet

Carla and Jan were not getting along. They had even stopped talking to each other. The time apart was starting to bother Carla. She and Jan had been best friends for years. She missed her.

"What should I do?" Carla asked Dad. "I want to be friends again. But I don't know if Jan does."

"I'm sure she does," answered Dad. "You girls need to bury the hatchet. Tell Jan how you feel. Let her know you're sorry and that you want to be friends again."

MEANING: To end a fight; to forgive someone

Catch-22

Nolan worried all the way home. Tomorrow was the school field trip to the zoo. But today his teacher told him some bad news. If Nolan didn't get all of his late assignments in, he wasn't going to be going. Tonight was Nolan's basketball game. He was an important player. He had to play, but he also had to finish his late assignments. Nolan explained the problem to Dad.

"I don't know what to tell you, Nolan," replied Dad. "It looks like a catch-22. Whatever you decide, you're going to have consequences."

MEANING: When you have a decision to make and neither choice is a good one; when there are negative or difficult things that will happen no matter what you decide

Caught red-handed

Pat saved his money and went to the store. He bought a bag of his favorite candy. He wasn't going to eat it all at once. He would make it last. A few days later, Pat looked at the bag. It was almost empty. He knew he hadn't been eating it that fast!

He went to his sister's bedroom. There she was, in the middle of her bed. Candy wrappers were everywhere.

"Tracy!" exclaimed Pat. "You're eating my candy. I've caught you red-handed!"

MEANING: To get caught doing something wrong

A chip on your shoulder

Lee was in a bad mood. He walked around all day with a frown on his face.

"Lee, would you help me with this?" asked his sister, Nora.

"Do it yourself," snapped Lee. "Can't you do anything for yourself?" He stomped out of the room.

Mom walked in a little later. "Where's Lee?" she asked.

"Outside," replied Nora. "But leave him alone. He's got a chip on his shoulder."

MEANING: To be in a bad mood and start fights or arguments on purpose

11

Dead as a doornail

Ted was excited to watch the tape of his baseball game. He popped the tape into the player and sat in his favorite chair. He grabbed the remote and started the tape. Nothing happened. He tried again. Still nothing happened.

"Dad!" called Ted. "What's wrong with the tape player?"

Dad came in and worked on the player. He tried everything. Dad finally looked at Ted.

"Sorry, Ted," said Dad. "You aren't going to watch your game tonight. That player is dead as a doornail."

MEANING: Not working at all; having no life or no chance of success

Down the hatch

Ellen didn't like peas. It didn't matter if they were boiled or mashed. She didn't like them hot, and she didn't like them cold. She let them sit until they were the very last thing on her plate.

"Ellen, hurry up and eat your peas. We want to go to the movies," said Mom.

Ellen scooped up all of the peas in one spoonful. "Down the hatch!" she said as she swallowed them all.

MEANING: To eat or swallow something, especially quickly or in one gulp

Easy as falling off a log

Izzy was watching television after school. She was feeling very lazy.

"Izzy," called her mom. "Where are you? I need you to finish folding these towels while I go get Mary from volleyball practice."

"Oh, Mom. I can't do that. It's too hard. I'll do it the wrong way," whined Izzy.

"Don't be silly," replied her mom. "I think you're just feeling lazy. What I want you to do is as easy as falling off a log. You can't possibly do it the wrong way."

MEANING: When something is very easy to do

Face the music

Theo was taking a long time walking home from school. He knew he was going to be in trouble. This was the fourth time that he didn't have his math assignment done. Last week his mom and dad had warned him that he would be grounded if he had any more late assignments. Theo couldn't see any way out of this one. He knew it was time to get home and face the music.

MEANING: To be brave and face a hard or uncomfortable situation; to accept responsibility for something you have done

A flash in the pan

Polly's team was on a losing streak. They had won their first two games but had lost the last five.

"Mom, what do you think the problem is?" asked Polly. "We were great in our first two games. Now we can't seem to win, no matter how hard we try!"

"I don't know, Polly. Maybe winning at first was just a flash in the pan," said Mom.

MEANING: To be successful for a very short time; to not have lasting success

Full of beans

Billy loved attention. He told jokes. He danced. He loved when people looked at him! At his grandpa's birthday party, Billy was the center of attention.

"Billy," said Grandpa with a laugh, "I can't keep up with you. I think you're full of beans!"

MEANING: To have lots of energy

Go fly a kite

Josh was getting fed up with his little brother, Kenny. He was trying to do his homework, and Kenny wouldn't stop bugging him! Josh finally shut his bedroom door so Kenny couldn't come in. Kenny whined out in the hall.

"Kenny!" exclaimed Josh. "Go fly a kite!"

MEANING: Leave me alone.

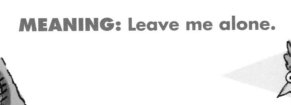

Have your cake and eat it too

Lily wanted a dog. She also wanted to go to the beach on summer vacation. Her family couldn't do both this year, so her parents told her to pick the thing she wanted the most. She decided on the beach vacation. After the trip, Lily's grandma called. Her mom answered the phone.

"Lily, we have a big surprise!" announced her mom. "Grandma is moving to an apartment. She can't keep her little dog, Charlie. Would you like to adopt him?" Lily could hardly believe it!

"It looks like you get to have your cake and eat it too, Lily!" exclaimed her mom.

MEANING: When you are supposed to pick between two things and end up with both

Ignorance is bliss

Mom was out of town for the weekend. While she was gone, the washer had sprung a leak. Everyone else had spent the weekend cleaning up the mess. When Mom got home on Sunday, she was greeted by her very tired family.

"How was your weekend?" asked Mom.

"Don't ask," answered Dad. "You missed all of the mess and work. You sure are lucky! Ignorance is bliss."

MEANING: Sometimes, you are happier not knowing about something that happened. You may be happier not getting bad news.

Keep a stiff upper lip

Gary and his dad sat in the doctor's office. Gary's ankle was swollen. It hurt a lot.

"Good news, Gary," said the doctor with a smile. "Your ankle isn't broken. Take it easy for a little while. I know it hurts right now, but keep a stiff upper lip. It will feel better before you know it!"

MEANING: To be brave; to not let others know that something is bothering you

Make ends meet

Cole knew his mother was worried. His father had just lost his job. Cole thought he might help by finding a job to make a little money for the family.

"Thank you, Cole," said Mom. "You don't need to worry, though. Things are a little tough right now, but we're making ends meet. Things will be fine."

MEANING: To have just enough money for the basic things you need

Miss the boat

Carlos was disappointed. He had been saving his money for a new red bike he had seen at the store. When he finally had enough money, he went to the store to get it. But the bike wasn't in the window! Carlos asked the store clerk about the bike.

"Sorry, you missed the boat," said the clerk. "We sold that bike last week."

MEANING: To miss a chance for something; to be late or miss out on something you really wanted or needed

18

On cloud nine

Bea was so happy. Tyler was going to the big dance with her. She had just picked out her dress. It was beautiful. Now she was planning all the other details. She was on cloud nine!

MEANING: To be very, very happy

Out of the blue

Morrie had been saving for new skis all year. In the summer he mowed lawns. In the fall he raked leaves. Now it was winter. He was shoveling walks and driveways. Morrie still didn't have enough money. He was getting worried. If he didn't start making money faster, winter would be over! Out of the blue, a letter came from Morrie's aunt. She had forgotten his birthday and sent him a late present! Inside the card was the money Morrie needed to buy his skis.

MEANING: When something unexpected happens

Pit stop

Ahmad's family had been driving for three hours. The drive was getting very long. They still had a few hours to go. Ahmad didn't think he could take one more minute of sitting still. Just then, his dad stopped the car at a restaurant.

"Time for a pit stop, everyone," said Dad with a smile. "We've all been sitting too long."

MEANING: To make a stop while riding in a vehicle

Pull your hair out

Mom was angry. She'd had a terrible day at work. One of the other workers spilled coffee on her important papers. The same worker typed the wrong thing into the computer and broke the telephone.

"That worker makes me so mad!" exclaimed Mom. "She just makes me want to pull my hair out!"

MEANING: To become angry or very frustrated

Read the riot act

Connor knew he and his brother were in big trouble. Dad had told them not to play football in the house. In fact, he'd told them a lot of times. Now the lamp was broken.

"Come on, Connor," said his brother. "Let's go tell Dad before he finds out on his own."

"I'm not looking forward to this," answered Connor. "You know he'll read us the riot act."

MEANING: To yell at someone or let them know how upset you are

A shot in the dark

"That test was hard!" exclaimed Mara. "I don't think I did very well."

"I thought it was OK," said Leo.

"You told me you didn't even study," said Mara. "How can you say it was OK? How did you even try answering the questions?"

"I just took a shot in the dark," answered Leo. "Hopefully I'll get lucky!"

MEANING: To try to do something when you aren't sure if you can be successful

Spill the beans

Mom had a special birthday coming up. Carly, her little brother, Jake, and her dad had been planning a special night.

"Dad, I'm worried about Jake," said Carly. "What if he tells Mom?"

"He knows this is a surprise, Carly," answered Dad.

"But," cried Carly, "it seems like every time Jake knows about a surprise, he spills the beans."

MEANING: To tell a secret

Through the grapevine

Rosa had been upset with her best friend, Sandy. She heard that Sandy was saying mean things about her. The two friends stopped talking. Then Rosa learned that the story about Sandy was untrue. A boy in their class made the story up just to cause trouble between the two friends. Now Rosa felt terrible. She asked her mom how to apologize to Sandy.

"I hope you have learned a lesson here," said Mom. "You have to be careful of what you hear through the grapevine. It's not always true."

MEANING: To receive information that has been passed on by many people

Turn the tables

Paul had been disappointed for the past three weeks. His friend Rob had gotten the lead in the class play. Paul only had a small part. But Paul tried to be happy. He worked hard to do his best at his small part.

But everything had changed today. Rob was sick, and the play was next week! Their teacher picked Paul to take Rob's place in the lead role. Paul ran home. He excitedly told his dad what had happened.

"Good for you, Paul!" said Dad. "I guess you turned the tables this time!"

MEANING: When a situation changes and becomes either much better or much worse

Ward County Public Library

A wet blanket

Ruth was very excited. Everyone was going to Jill's sleepover party. There would be movies, pizza and lots of fun. Ruth rushed home to ask her dad if she could go.

"Ruth," said her dad. "You've got an early morning practice tomorrow. I hate to be a wet blanket, but we can't have you tired for such a big day."

MEANING: To say no to something; to ruin someone's fun

X marks the spot

Joan's family was hosting the neighborhood Fourth-of-July picnic. Everyone was working hard to get everything ready. The biggest project was to put up the flagpole. Joan's dad got all the supplies ready to go.

"Come on, everyone. We're ready to dig the hole!" he called. "Here's a shovel, Joan. You can be first to start digging."

"Where do I start?" asked Joan.

"Right here," answered her dad. "X marks the spot!"

MEANING: The spot where something should go or where something is placed

Ward County Public Library

WARD COUNTY PUBLIC -LIBRARY
MINOT, NORTH DAKOTA

FOR RENEWAL, CALL: 852-5388
OR TOLL FREE: 1-800-932-8932
KENMARE BRANCH: 385-4090